THE GENTLE ART OF SWEDISH DEATH CLEANING

*How to Free Yourself and Your
Family from a Lifetime of Clutter*

Text and Drawings by

MARGARETA MAGNUSSON

SCRIBNER

New York   London   Toronto   Sydney   New Delhi

Scribner
An Imprint of Simon & Schuster, Inc.
1230 Avenue of the Americas
New York, NY 10020

First Scribner hardcover edition January 2018

SCRIBNER and design are registered trademarks of The Gale Group, Inc., used under license by Simon & Schuster, Inc., the publisher of this work.

For information about special discounts for bulk purchases, please contact Simon & Schuster Special Sales at 1-866-506-1949 or business@simonandschuster.com.

The Simon & Schuster Speakers Bureau can bring authors to your live event. For more information or to book an event, contact the Simon & Schuster Speakers Bureau at 1-866-248-3049 or visit our website at www.simonspeakers.com.

Designed by Jill Putorti

Manufactured in the United States of America

10 9

Library of Congress Cataloging-in-Publication Data is available.

Excerpt from "A Gazelle" © Frans G. Bengtsson

ISBN 978-1-5011-7324-0
ISBN 978-1-5011-7325-7 (ebook)

To my five children

"Putting your house in order, if you can do it, is one of the most comforting activities, and the benefits of it are incalculable."

—LEONARD COHEN, *THE NEW YORKER*

CONTENTS

FOREWORD

The only thing we know for sure is that we will die one day. But before that we can try to do almost anything.

You have probably been given this little book by one of your children, or as a gift from someone in the same situation as you and me.

Or perhaps you've picked up a copy for yourself, because it struck a chord. There is a reason for this. You have collected so much wonderful stuff in your life—stuff that your family and friends can't evaluate or take care of.

Let me help make your loved ones' memories of you nice—instead of awful.

MM

DEATH CLEANING
IS NOT SAD

I am death cleaning, or, as we call it in Swedish, *döstädning*.

Dö is "death" and *städning* is "cleaning." In Swedish it is a term that means that you remove unnecessary things and make your home nice and orderly when you think the time is coming closer for you to leave the planet.

It is so important that I have to tell you about it. Maybe I can also give you a few tips, since this is something that we will all have to face sooner or later. We really must if we want to save precious time for our loved ones after we are gone.

So what is death cleaning? For me it means going through all my belongings and deciding how to get rid of the things I do not want anymore. Just look around you. Several of your things have probably been there for so long that you do not even see or value them anymore.

I think the term *döstädning* is quite new, but not the act of *döstädning*. It is a word that is used when you or

MARGARETA MAGNUSSON/

someone else does a good, thorough cleaning and gets rid of things to make life easier and less crowded. It does not necessarily have to do with your age or death, but often does. Sometimes you just realize that you can hardly close your drawers or barely shut your closet door. When that happens, it is definitely time to do something, even if you are only in your thirties. You could call that kind of cleaning *döstädning*, too, even if you may be many, many years away from dying.

I think women have always death cleaned, but women's work is not often in the spotlight, and should be appreciated more. When it comes to death cleaning, in my generation and those older than me, women tend to clean up after their husbands first, and then they clean up before they themselves are no more. While one would usually say "clean up *after* yourself," here we are dealing with the odd situation of cleaning up *before* . . . we die.

Some people can't wrap their heads around death. And these people leave a mess after them. Did they think they were immortal?

Many adult children do not want to talk about death with their parents. They should not be afraid. We must all talk about death. If it's too hard to address, then death cleaning can be a way to start the conversation.

The other day, I told one of my sons that I was death

cleaning and writing a book about it. He wondered if it was going to be a sad book and whether it made me sad to write it.

No, no, I said. It is not sad at all. Neither the cleaning nor the writing of the book.

Sometimes I feel a little uncomfortable with how unappreciative I am being about some of the things I want to rid myself of. Some of these things have brought benefits to me.

But I've discovered that it is rewarding to spend time with these objects one last time and then dispose of them. Each item has its own history, and remembering that history is often enjoyable. When I was younger, I never used to have the time to sit and think about what an object meant to me in my life, or where it came from, or when and how it came into my possession. The difference between death cleaning and just a big cleanup is the amount of time they consume. Death cleaning is not about dusting or mopping up; it is about a permanent form of organization that makes your everyday life run more smoothly.

Now, when I am not running around Stockholm, taking part in all that the city has to offer, I have time to take part in all that my apartment has to offer, which is a reflection of my life.

The world is a worried place. Floods, volcanic eruptions, earthquakes, fires, and wars follow one another. To listen to the media or read newspapers makes me depressed. I would shrivel up if I could not get relief from the negativity of the world's news with good friends, experiences out in the natural world, music, beautiful things, or just enjoying something as simple as a sunny day (which can be rare in our northern climate).

I would never, ever want to write something sad; there is enough sadness out there already. So I hope you will find the words and thoughts ahead helpful, entertaining, perhaps even a bit humorous.

To do your own death cleaning can really be very hard. Maybe you have to downsize your home for some reason, maybe you have become single, or perhaps you need to move to a nursing home. These situations tend to affect most of us.

Going through all your old belongings, remembering when you used them last, and hopefully saying good-bye to several of them is very difficult for many of us. People tend to hoard rather than throw away.

I have death cleaned so many times for others, I'll be damned if someone else has to death clean after me.

Once someone is gone, there can be chaos enough anyway, I can tell you. There are many sad stories about siblings who start to quarrel because they want the same item. This type of situation does not need to happen; we can plan in advance to lessen the chances of these unhappy moments.

I had, for example, a very nice bracelet that my father gave to my mother a long time ago. It was given to me in my mother's will. The easiest way to avoid future complications among my children was to sell it! That was a very good idea, I think.

Later, discussing the sale with my children, they were fine with my decision. They had each been given something that had belonged to my father and mother. And after all, the bracelet was mine to do with as I pleased. Taking precious time to discuss one bracelet with my five children seemed unreasonable. Death cleaning is about saving such time.

WHY I AM WRITING THIS BOOK

I am now somewhere between eighty and one hundred years old. I take it as a responsibility of my old age to tell you about my experiences, because I believe this philosophy of death cleaning is important for all of us to know. It doesn't matter if it is your parents, friends, or family who are getting older or if it is about time for you to begin death cleaning for yourself.

I have moved seventeen times within my own country and abroad so I should know what I am talking about when it comes to deciding what to keep and what to throw away, whether you are moving house, moving country, or moving to the Great Beyond!

Although it seems to be mostly women who death clean, since they statistically live longer than their husbands or partners, sometimes, like in the family in which I grew up, my father was left alone first.

If someone has lived in a home for many years where children, grown-ups, relatives, and guests have stayed and felt welcome, that same someone is often so busy that they never think of reducing the number of things in the household.

And so the number of possessions grows and collects quickly over the years. Suddenly the situation is out of control and the weight of all those things can begin to seem tiring.

Your exhaustion with all this stuff may appear out of the blue one day. When someone cancels a weekend visit or a dinner, you feel grateful—instead of disappointed—because you may be too tired to clean up for their visit. The problem is that you have too much stuff to deal with. It is time to change your way of living. It is never too late to start!

PRECIOUS TIME AND HELPING PARENTS

Today things are very different from when I was young, of course. I did not say *better*. But the pace today is very fast. Many young families have to schedule their lives down to the smallest increment to have time to do what they consider most important.

Do not ever imagine that anyone will wish—or be able—to schedule time off to take care of what you didn't bother to take care of yourself. No matter how much they love you, don't leave this burden to them.

The first time I came across death cleaning was when I had to empty my parents' apartment after the death of my mother. My parents had been married for forty-six years and my father was not capable of taking care of everything himself when moving to a smaller apartment. Together we picked out the furniture, linens, household utensils, knickknacks, and paintings that would make his new home nice and comfortable.

My mother had been a very orderly, wise, and realistic woman. She had been sick for some time, and I believe she suspected she did not have a very long time to live and had therefore started to plan ahead for after her death.

As I began to clean up their home, I found messages attached to clothes and many other things: small handwritten instructions as to what should be done with everything. Some parcels were assigned to charity, some books were to be returned to their original owners. An old horse-riding suit should go to the Museum of History, said a note fastened with a pin on one of the jacket lapels. There was also the name of whom I should contact at the museum.

Even if these small instructions were not addressed specifically to me, I felt consoled by them. I felt that my mother was there for me. She really had done some of her own death cleaning. I was grateful, and it has proven to be a very good example for me of how to take responsibility for your things to make it easier on your loved ones after your death.

My five children were between one and eleven years old at the time, so I was very busy. Because I had so little time, we decided to work with an auctioneer to clean out the house and to sell anything that my father did not want or need in his new, smaller home. An auctioneer may sound expensive and a little exclusive but it really isn't. The auctioneer's commission is deducted from the items that are sold, so it was no cash out of my pocket or my father's. Under the circumstances, it was the best option for us.

Auction houses are generally very helpful if you do not have friends or siblings to help you.

The auctioneer's office had to take care of a lot. I remember that as soon as they started, it all went very fast.

I had to stop some of the movers carrying things down the stairs before the objects disappeared out of my sight forever. But I didn't take it too much to heart if a few too many things went to the auctioneers. I had many things to take care of that were more urgent and complicated, such as my children's needs, my father's state of mind about the move, and our grief over the loss of his wife, my mother. It was just not the time to be overly concerned with material things.

And besides, I had made sure that we had the basic things my father would need, such as household utensils and furniture. If a few too many things went to auction, it was not the end of the world. The most important was to hold on to the things that my father wanted to have in his new apartment. We kept his beloved desk (where he placed a portrait of my mother), his favorite chair, and a few paintings he did not want to part with.

HOW TO BEGIN

How to begin?

Be aware of the fact that to downsize your home will take some time. Old people seem to think time goes so quickly, but in fact it is we who have become slower. So— do not wait too long. . . .

This new job of yours will not be accomplished any faster if you wait, but with a little practice and preparation, it will certainly be easier for you to make decisions about how to get rid of things. Trust me, the more time you spend going through your belongings, the easier it will be for you to decide what to keep and what not to. The more you work at it, the less time-consuming it will become. You might even discover the added bonus that it will feel wonderful to visit a dump and throw worthless things as far as you are able to.

Start by checking the basement or the attic or the cupboards by your front door. These areas are great places to temporarily get rid of your excess. Temporarily—well, many of the things you have in storage have probably been standing there for ages. You may even have forgotten what it is you have there. Good for you, because you will now realize that you will not miss anything if you throw it away.

Visit these storage areas and start pulling out what's hidden there. It may be a dollhouse or ice-hockey equipment, mostly things that you yourself did not want around anymore. Sometimes your attic has become so full that you are forced to put things in someone else's attic! Terrible! Who do you think will take care of that later when you are no longer here?

Tell your loved ones and friends what you are up to. They might want to help you and even take things you don't need and also help you to move things that you cannot move alone. You will see that a steady stream of people you like (or even dislike) will come to take things such as books, clothes, and utensils.

Perhaps a grandchild or someone else you know is about to move into their first apartment. Invite them over and you can show them your things and chat about them, telling them stories about the objects (or perhaps even your life) that they do not know. Meanwhile, have some bags and boxes at hand that you can fill while you are chatting, so they can take stuff with them right away.

A SMALL PIECE OF ADVICE

Don't start with photographs—or letters and personal papers, for that matter.

It can be both a lot of fun and a bit sad to go through photographs and letters, but one thing is certain: if you start with them, you will definitely get stuck down memory lane and may never get around to cleaning anything else.

Pictures and letters that you have saved for some reason must wait until you have arranged the destinies for your furniture and other belongings. In general, when death cleaning, size really matters. Start with the large items in your home, and finish with the small. Photographs carry such a weight of emotion that they will hinder your work, but are also so important that they have their own chapter later in this book.

WHAT TO KEEP AND WHAT NOT TO

The intention is not that we should remove things that make our lives pleasant and more comfortable.

But if you can't keep track of your things, then you know you have too many.

I feel comfortable in a home that is reasonably orderly. I don't want anything that my eyes do not like. If I have a beautiful chair, I am not going to put my dirty laundry on it. There must be something wrong with the way I have organized my home if I have to continually mess up the place that I originally worked so hard to decorate and keep orderly.

Life will become more pleasant and comfortable if we get rid of some of the abundance.

SORT AND SORT OUT

When you look at your home, you probably see a bunch of objects that have only one thing in common: they belong to you. But in fact, most things you own have many things in common. Almost everything in our homes belongs to different categories. You can classify them as furniture, clothes, books, linen, for example.

There are of course many different categories in different homes. Golfers, gardeners, sailors, football players— all have different inventories. Some of these categories are more difficult to handle when it comes to removing things from your home.

Choose a category that you believe is easy for you to handle. An easy category is one with many items to choose from and without too much sentimental connection.

It is important that your first choice is easy for you. I do not want you to give up immediately.

When you have managed to go through a couple of categories you will feel so good. Very soon your home will become so much easier to look after. I am sure that your family and friends will encourage you to carry on.

I always choose clothes as my first category. That is easy for me since I know that I have many garments in my wardrobe that I seldom or never use.

When I have death cleaned for other people, such as my parents, my husband, or my mother-in-law, I always started with clothes. They are often so specific in size that unless you know a friend or loved one who is roughly the same size, it is best to give all the clothes away.

But if you are starting with your own wardrobe, sort all your clothes into two piles (on your bed or on a table).

Pile 1 is for clothes you want to keep.

Pile 2 is for clothes you want to get rid of.

Then look through pile 1 and pull out items that require small adjustments or dry cleaning. The rest you can put back in the closet.

Give or throw away the clothes in pile 2.

When I saw my piles of clothes, I could not believe that I had bought all of this. But I guess that birthday presents and Christmas gifts have added to the quantity. Some things were too small, some too big. If your figure has changed a lot over the last year, I would add garments that no longer fit to pile 2.

After having looked through the lot one time, I managed to reduce my wardrobe by two dresses, five scarves, one jacket, and two pairs of shoes. A grandchild took a pair of shoes and the rest I gave to the Red Cross. Wonderful!

Our society more or less requires that we dress ourselves for different occasions. For every day, for festivities, for happiness, and for sorrow. We also must remember that our clothes help us to adjust ourselves to different seasons and work environments.

Perhaps you are among those who are lucky enough to have a so-called walk-in closet, but if so, you will of course also be unlucky as you will have more clothing to air out, wash, and take care of . . . and later to dispose of.

When I was young, I read a great article on how to arrange a low-maintenance closet. The point was that it is not the amount of clothing that makes a person well-dressed. The article was all about choosing clothing carefully and then organizing it well. I've actually lived with this advice for the rest of my life. In the closet, as with everywhere else in your home, it is all about organization—so that you can quickly and easily find something suitable when you need it.

In my opinion, all garments in a closet should look good together, and you should be able to mix and exchange them with one another.

Now, if you must reduce your wardrobe, it is good to take a few hours to go through it thoroughly to see what you can actually do without. There are certainly impulse purchases and other things that do not really go with any other garments—when you look at your wardrobe as a whole, these are often easy to spot. Only keep those that you really feel you will wear or if the sentimental connection is very strong. Sometimes a shock of color or pattern against a simpler palette can indeed be refreshing to the eye, and a joy to wear.

I have a jacket that fits everywhere and nowhere. I bought it from a lady in a market in China many decades ago. It is a patchwork of many pieces of fabric and has embroidery representing funny fantasy animals. It is so colorful and carefully stitched together. A piece of joy made from recycled materials by someone imaginative. Was it the little lady in the market who made it? Maybe. I want to save this jacket because it makes me happy and I wear it on Christmas Eve.

But this is not a style manual. . . . We must keep investigating: cleaning, organizing, and sorting!

MORE ORGANIZING

It is always much easier to death clean a home when it is well organized. By "organized," I mean that all things have a place of their own. When your home is a complete mess, it is very hard to clean it at all. But it is never too late to do something about this problem. While you ponder where this thing you are holding in your hand belongs, perhaps you will find that you don't need this thing at all.

Where I live we have a club called Senior Net. It is a place where retired people or really anyone above the age of fifty-five with limited computer skills can get help with their computer problems from other retired, but more capable seniors. My helper was not happy with the disorder of my computer files.

He looked at the screen and said:

"This is like putting your toilet in the kitchen."

So he helped me. He organized my files. I was seventy-nine years old at the time, but I got the help I needed and afterward it was much easier for me to find my way through my computer.

The same can happen to you, in your home; you don't even need a computer to realize this. I was just making a comparison, because in a computer everything is assorted and organized.

IT IS NO FUN TO PLAY "HIDE THE KEY" WHEN YOU HAVE HIDDEN IT FROM YOURSELF

When my children were young, we had birthday parties where we used to play a Swedish game called *gömma nyckeln*, or "hide the key." Oh, what fun that was! I would hide the key—a big old key from the seventeenth century—somewhere in our home and then let the kids loose. It was like hide-and-go-seek without some poor child having to hide in a cupboard and be forgotten. So I hid the key, and when any of the children came close to the little treasure I would shout:

"It is getting warmer!"

Too far from it I would say:

"It is getting colder!"

Such joy it was to play that game. But as an adult, it is no fun at all when you wake up in the morning and cannot find your glasses. And nobody says, "It is getting warmer" when you look for them. Organize!

In a home where you have been living for some time, it should be easy to keep some order.

Still, I know families who live in a complete mess (I won't mention the names of my children here, but you know who you are). Mess is an unnecessary source of irritation. Even in a fairly small family, one or several members wander about looking for keys, gloves, certificates, or cell phones. Whatever.

All these things have something in common! They should, but don't yet, have a place of their own. Give everything a place and you won't feel angry, irritated, or desperate when leaving the house. You will not as often stand by the front door yelling, "Where are my whatevers?" And for a change—and as an added bonus—you may also arrive on time.

Most people clean their homes once a week. When you go through your home with the vacuum cleaner or mop, you will probably find things that belong somewhere else. Gloves on the piano, the hairbrush in the kitchen, a set of keys on the sofa . . .

Bring a bag with you as you clean the house, or wear an apron with a huge pocket. Whenever you see something that is not where it should be, put it in the apron pocket or in the bag. When you are finished, you can show everything you have collected to the people you live with and ask them to put their things back where they belong. Some households have so many misplaced items that a bag or an apron pocket isn't big enough. These households need immediate organization. I have always organized my homes and cleared my clutter, so an apron with a pocket works for me. My apron is very stylish with a nice leopard pattern; it is such a nice apron that I almost want to wear it all the time, even when I go out for dinner.

In a hallway it is always good to have hooks for keys on a wall and some baskets or boxes for gloves, hats, and scarves. If you live in a house with several floors, it saves time to place a basket on the landing of every floor for things that have to go up or down. But make sure never to put your foot in the basket.

Once, about ten years ago, I went on a sailing trip with

a family for several days. Whenever everybody on board was to leave the boat for an hour or more, the cabin door needed to be locked, but no one could ever find the key from when we had last unlocked the door. Who had the key? Who had it the last time? Beautiful islands were around us, and yet every adventure off the boat began with a bad mood that affected us all and was always caused by the hunt for the key! Imagine how a little hook for the key on the inside of the cabin door could have brightened our lives on board.

Sometimes the smallest changes can have amazing effects. If you find yourself repeatedly having the same problem, fix it!

A hook costs nothing.

A VERY GOOD APPROACH

The second time I came across death cleaning was when my mother-in-law died. She had already moved to a much smaller apartment and had managed to get rid of most of the things she did not have use for anymore. Her small apartment always looked beautiful, nice, and cozy.

My mother-in-law knew a woman who came to help with the things she could not manage to do herself. My mother-in-law called her Snow White. We never caught a glimpse of any dwarves, but Snow White possessed many of their hardworking qualities.

My children—her grandchildren, who were in their first small adult apartments—loved to visit their grandmother. She used to cook dinner for them and tell them about the time when she and their grandfather lived in Japan many years before, when he had worked for the Swedish Match Company.

In the depths of the Depression, my mother-in-law and father-in-law and their son (my husband, born in 1932) had to return home to Sweden.

My mother-in-law was really a very capable and gifted woman. Returning from Japan to Sweden in the 1930s, she opened a small boutique on the city's main street. There she sold silk, china, beautiful lacquer work, baskets, and other things imported from Japan. I believe she was the first Swedish person who used baskets for something other than laundry and picking mushrooms. She would use a basket for beautiful flower arrangement, for example—a style that is now very common and much used (you place a vase or any suitable container in the basket so that you can pour some water in it for the flowers).

Very soon the upper-class women found their way to her shop, which she had called Mt. Fuji. My mother-in-law had many pleasant and unpleasant stories about how she was treated by certain "fine ladies" when she served them from behind the counter.

In the last years of her life, every time we visited her or when she came to us, she would give us beautiful china plates, a pretty tablecloth, or nicely colored napkins to take home, pressing them into our hands as we left. That went on for many years before she made her last move to the small apartment that would be her final home. It was her method of death cleaning: over time she had slowly and unobtrusively given a lot away in a quiet, kind way. At the same time she had added beautiful and useful things to her friends' and loved ones' homes.

At that time, I never realized how thoughtful she was. Of course there were still things to take care of in spite of her thoughtfulness, but many fewer things than there might have been. Even today I feel grateful that she made it so much easier for us when she died.

HAPPY PEOPLE

I know many people who can sit in a messy home and look as if they are happy and in harmony. To me they seem almost comical. I don't understand them.

I sometimes feel envious, as I myself cannot feel happy at all in a home that looks as if it has been tumble-dried.

When our gang of kids swelled to five in only ten years' time, we rearranged the main entrance of our home to resemble a Swedish preschool. Every child had their own color, a cubby in that color, and a clothes hook of their own. All their outdoor clothes were hung on the hook, or put away in the little cubbies. The kids' outdoor gear never entered the living area. To hang one's jacket on a hook and put the mittens in their place does not take much more time than to throw them on the floor. And the best thing is that the kids could find their things on their own, never having to ask, "Mom, have you seen my . . ."

To hunt for misplaced things is never an effective use of your time.

So, work to keep things organized throughout your life, and death cleaning will be easier for everyone. Your loved ones will not be happy people when they have to do your organizing for you.

A SECOND OPINION

If you decide to downsize your home on your own, you may want to talk to someone about it, someone who isn't family and doesn't have a sentimental connection to the items you want to get rid of.

Maybe you want some advice or just other viewpoints from someone who is in a similar situation (other than me), or from someone much younger. Preferably they will think differently from you, and that is good. That will help you look at your work—or even other dilemmas—from fresh angles.

Ask these people to come over if you do not live too far from each other. Do not forget to write down a list of all the things you want their advice about. Nobody wants to wait around while you are searching for the questions you had in your mind. The following are some of the questions I have had when death cleaning:

Which charity is best to donate books to?
*This painting has no real value but is very pretty, will
     anyone want it?*
Can I give an old samurai sword to my teenage grandson?

Not huge or difficult questions, but questions that could do with a second opinion.

MY THIRD DEATH CLEANING

The third time I undertook the challenge of death cleaning, it was not in someone else's house, but my own. My husband of forty-eight years died after a long illness, and I was struggling to both clean up all his things and to begin thinking of how to organize my own things for my move to a smaller living space.

When you have been a couple for many years, it is hard to handle the fact that you have become single. Your favorite oracle and problem solver is no longer around. He will never show up again to keep you company and to make life easier. This is a terrible fact that we each encounter in different ways, whether it is a spouse, or the inevitable loss of our closest friend or family members.

I tried to present myself as I believed that other people wanted to see me: that I was not going to break down and that I was working hard to move on.

And yet, in a way, my dearest and best friend was still very present in our home, which made it hard to move on. I realized that I had to find a new home quickly, a place where there would be fewer memories and that would be more manageable for one person to look after—preferably without a big garden or too many stairs and rooms to clean. I no longer enjoyed or was capable of mowing the lawn or shoveling snow . . . or interested in dusting, for that matter.

To compress the contents of a roomy home with a spacious garden into a two-room apartment with a balcony is not done in a few hours. My grown-up children claimed some clothes, books, tools, and furniture, but of course a lot of things remained to take care of, to sort, to keep, or to throw away.

I contacted an official valuer, who looked at the things I wanted to get rid of and gave me an appraisal. Some of these things I put up for sale. I then asked friends and neighbors to come over and see if there was anything they wanted. After that, I went into each room and made a list of everything that was left in the room, and made a clear note of what to do with each item. Next to a lamp I would write "give to Peter," next to a painting "give to Aunt

Ellen," next to something I couldn't place with a person I knew, I would write "give to a charity."

With all of this done, I allotted each room in my home one week to clear up. In this way, I felt I could handle the death cleaning on my own, without rushing. Some spaces like the laundry room would not take a whole week of course, but there would be more time left to do other things around the house that would make leaving and selling it much easier.

After each room was done I took a well-deserved break.

DEATH CLEANING ON YOUR OWN

It would have been incredibly nice to have had my husband's company to help me get through emptying our home, my third death cleaning. But it was impossible. He was dead.

All my kids came home for the funeral, but the death cleaning took almost a year. I worked at a steady pace on my own. I kept in mind comments from my children about certain objects they adored and held on to these items to give to them later, while cleaning out other things that nobody cared about.

If I had asked my children and their spouses for assistance, I am sure they would have done their utmost to help me. But I did not ask. Three of them had small children and they had jobs in places such as the United States, Africa, and Japan, far from my little house on the west coast of Sweden. It would have been too much to organize a visit from my children and their children and all their bags. Besides, I hate to ask for help.

To go through all the things that documented our life together (fifty years of ups mostly, some downs, five kids) by myself made me feel very lonely. My husband and I should have done the job together, starting at sixty-five, maybe even earlier when we were stronger and our health was better. But everyone thinks they will live forever. Suddenly, my soul mate was gone.

In hindsight, I think that doing it on my own might have been a good thing. Perhaps it was easier for me to do by myself.

Had I cleaned with my husband, it would have taken us years. Men tend to save most things rather than throw them away. That goes for even the smallest nuts and bolts. They think, and rightly so sometimes, that every little thing will be useful at some later occasion.

And had my kids shown up, they would have wanted to save everything. Everything! Or at least they would have had different, confusing opinions on what to save.

So in the end the best thing really was to do the cleaning myself. On the other hand, if you have children who have huge amounts of time on their hands, by all means involve them in your cleaning.

HOW TO DISCUSS THE
TOPIC OF DEATH CLEANING

When I was young, it was not really deemed polite to speak your mind to an older person, including your own parents. It was especially frowned upon for younger people to discuss topics that older people hadn't asked their opinion about first. To be outspoken and honest was regarded as impolite.

That is why the adults at that time—my parents' generation and their parents before them—didn't have the faintest idea what young people thought about anything. The parents and children didn't understand one another as well as they might have. It was very stupid really and sad, a missed opportunity for the different generations to know each other better. And death and preparing for death were not usually discussed.

Today, we often believe that honesty is more important than politeness. At best, we combine the two. I don't think that younger people today are as "tactful" and reserved as my generation was, and that can be a good thing for everyone. Tact can be an important value so as not to hurt someone's feelings, but since we all must—one day or another—look death clearly in the face, perhaps tact does not have much place in the discussions we all must find a way to have.

Today we can more easily say to parents, or anyone, really, "What are you going to do with all your things when you do not have the strength for or the interest in taking care of them anymore?"

Many adult children worry about the amount of possessions their parents have amassed through the years. They know that if their parents don't take care of their own stuff, they, the children, will have to do it for them.

If your parents are getting old and you don't know how to bring up the topic of what to do with all the stuff, I would suggest you pay them a visit, sit down, and ask some of the following questions in a gentle way:

"You have many nice things, have you thought about what you want to do with it all later on?"

"Do you enjoy having all this stuff?"

"Could life be easier and less tiring if we got rid of some of this stuff that you have collected over the years?"

"Is there anything we can do together in a slow way so that there won't be too many things to handle later?"

Old people often have a problem with their balance. Rugs, stacks of books on the floor, and odd items lying about the house can be safety hazards. Perhaps this can be a way to start your discussion. Ask about the rugs. Are they really safe?

Perhaps this is where "tact" is still important, to ask these questions in as gentle and caring a way as you can. It is possible that the first few times you ask, your parents may want to avoid the topic, or change the subject, but it is important to open the discussion. If you are unable to get them to talk with you, then leave them to think and return a few weeks or a few months later and ask again, perhaps in a slightly different way.

Or ask them over the phone or mention that there are certain things in their house that you would like to have and could you perhaps take them now? Maybe they will be relieved to get rid of a few things, and that will help them to begin to see the promise and possible enjoyment of beginning to death clean for themselves.

If you are too scared to be a little "impolite" with your parents and you do not dare to raise the topic or ask them questions to help them think about how they want to handle their things, don't be surprised if you get stuck with it all later on!

A loved one wishes to inherit *nice* things from you. Not *all* things from you.

DID THE VIKINGS KNOW THE REAL SECRET OF DEATH CLEANING?

Sometimes I think it must have been much easier to live and die at the time of our ancestors, the Vikings.

When they buried their relatives, they also buried many objects together with the body. This was to be sure that the dead would not miss anything in their new environment. It was also an assurance for the family members who remained that they would not become obsessed with spirits of the dead and constantly be reminded of them because their possessions were still scattered all over the tent or mud hut. Very clever.

Can you imagine the same scenario today? With all the *skräp* (Swedish for "junk") people have now, they would have to be buried in Olympic-sized swimming pools so that their stuff could go with them!

ONLY COUNT THE HAPPY MOMENTS

There is a line that Anni-Frid Lyngstad from ABBA used to sing: "Only count the happy moments, and forget the ones that cause you sorrow." It is damned important to make time for the happy moments that will become good memories later on.

Sweden has a very long coastline, and sailing is very popular in our country. In our family we used to sail and talk about sailing a lot. Very often our dinners would turn into veritable sailing races.

Many pieces of the cutlery were turned into boats in our imagination. Forks and spoons struck at one another, and the mustard pot became a rounding mark. It was a big fight to reach the finish line between the pepper mill and the saltshaker.

We talked about the latest race and we laughed about our shortcomings as sailors and, later, remembering my husband, the kids' father, we cried as well.

When I was preparing to leave my house, I asked my grown-up kids if anyone wanted the table on which so many imaginary sailing races had taken place. All of them said no.

Luckily, just when I was about to donate the table, one of my children suddenly got a new apartment and needed a table, so there it is today. I am happy that this child will remember the happy races at that table and perhaps create new ones with his own loved ones.

Still, it would have been a nice table for someone else's home if a family member had not taken it. You can always hope and wait for someone to want something in your home, but you cannot wait forever, and sometimes you must just give cherished things away with the wish that they end up with someone who will create new memories of their own.

THE LITTLE OPTIMIST

A few years after our children left home, we still had a small wooden boat that we had used to teach them how to sail with while they were growing up. The little boat wasn't in the way and we didn't really want to get rid of it, partly because it held so many fond sailing memories, and partly because we thought it would be a fun thing to use for a new generation should we have grandchildren. We wanted to keep the little boat around.

In our backyard there was a typically Swedish red barn

with white doors and window trim. Under the barn's roof, the small boat found shelter to wait for those grandchildren. A wooden boat is sensitive; the barn was not too humid nor too dry and so the boat waited patiently for a number of years, carefully looked after by the barn.

In the end, it turned out that none of the grandchildren thought sailing was especially fun, and so we sold the boat. We were sad. Though they were all sent to sailing school, most of them only enjoyed the lessons where they learned what to do when the boat capsizes and they have to survive in the water. That was a good lesson for them to learn, but the actual sailing part of the lessons never caught on or appealed to them.

The boat was a type called an Optimist dinghy. It is a beginner's boat. If that little boat had been able to speak, no one would have believed all the stories it could have told: tales of victory and defeat, tales of oceans and islands and fjords it had brought its occupants to.

I particularly remember a car trip to France for a sailing competition. We had our five children with us, a friend of theirs, and four little Optimist dinghies. One was on the roof of the car and three were on a trailer behind the car. When we reached Ghent in Belgium, it was dark out and we didn't know which route to take to reach our destination.

We saw a police officer on a motorcycle parked on the

roadside. My husband stopped the car, rolled down the window, and asked for directions. The policeman looked at our load of sailboats and at all the curious little kids in the car. He blew his whistle and suddenly three more policemen on motorcycles turned up. With two motorcycles in front, and two behind us, we were escorted through town. Can you imagine how thrilled we were? None of this would have happened without that little boat (and its friends).

So, understandably, it was difficult for us to get rid of the boat. But what we learned from this is not to hang on to things that nobody seems to want.

A WOMAN'S JOB

I sometimes wonder how men cope when they become widowed.

Men of my generation often manage poorly, especially if they had wives who spoiled them. They can barely boil an egg, let alone sew on a button. My husband could cope with most small daily things like simple cooking and mending. My father, who was a doctor, could clean the fish he caught very nicely; it almost looked like he had operated on them. The fillets were guaranteed to be boneless! But could he cook them? Nope.

For a long time, the best solution for widowers has been to get a new wife as quickly as possible—someone to do the laundry and ironing, and to save them from impending starvation.

I think that the next generations of men will be better able to cope if they are widowed. In Sweden, many young men enjoy both sewing and knitting; others are fantastic cooks and can combine flavors that make the mouth sing! And they are not so stupid as to waste time ironing the entire shirt when they intend to wear a sweater on top; they know that only collar and cuffs count. When these younger generations get old, their skills will be of great benefit to them.

I guess death cleaning has traditionally been a woman's job. Women have been in charge of the home and have also tended to live longer. We have often also been the ones who clean up after our children and our husbands, so we are used to cleaning.

Women of my generation were brought up to not be in the way, to not trouble their surroundings with their presence. That is not the case with men, who take the space they are given for granted. My daughter sometimes says that I am so worried about being a nuisance that my worry itself becomes troublesome. Men don't think like I do, but they should. They, too, can be in the way.

DON'T FORGET YOURSELF

While death cleaning, you must not forget to take care of your present life: your home, maybe the garden, and yourself.

If you decide to downsize your home, it is a good thing not to be in a hurry. If possible, you should take your time and proceed at a pace that suits you. It will be absorbing but also tiring sometimes, but it is important that you don't overdo it.

When you remember the money you are saving by doing it yourself, and all the time you will save your family and friends who will not have to do it for you, it will really make you feel that the work you are doing is worth it.

Also, maybe you—as I did—will realize how many valuable things you have in your possession and that you want to let other people have them so they can enjoy and take care of them.

However, now is not the time to get stuck in memories. No, now planning for your future is much more important. Look forward to a much easier and calmer life—you will love it!

Regard your cleaning as an ordinary, everyday job. And in between, enjoy yourself as much as possible with all the things you like to do. With friends, charity, walking, playing boules or cards. An acquaintance of mine complained that it is no fun to play bridge when two of the gang of four have left the earth. That is of course sad. But young people are also nice to meet and play with, and they value your friendship as you value theirs. Besides, they do not talk about hearing aids and other sad things all the time.

You will probably also need to use some of your time to see the optician, the dentist, and your doctor for health checkups and more. Those also take time.

While death cleaning I have gotten to know some very interesting, funny, and nice people when I have contacted auctioneers, antiques dealers, secondhand shops, and charity organizations.

Aging is certainly not for weaklings. That is why you should not wait too long to start your downsizing. Sooner or later you will have your own infirmities, and then it is damn nice to be able to enjoy the things you can still manage to do without the burden of too many things to look after and too many messes to organize.

Sometimes I do miss my garden very much. But I must say it is much easier to just enjoy someone else's garden. (And if someone wants to learn or talk about gardening, they can ask you and listen: you still have the knowledge.)

MAKING THE MOVE TO A SMALLER SPACE

I read recently in an American newspaper of a whole new group of people who can be hired to help older people shrink their belongings and organize their new, smaller spaces in the way they would like. I think it is a good idea, but when I saw what these people were charging, I worried at what the final bill would be: careful, thoughtful death cleaning takes many, many hours.

Hiring a specialist like this may also make the process go so fast (because you do not want to have to pay for too many hours!) that you do not get the peace of mind you need to really think over and plan your next home. Do not forget that you may live for many years to come. That is a good reason to go through your belongings carefully and ponder what furniture, textiles, books, paintings, lamps, etc., you want to keep.

There are of course many ways to go about this. Maybe you have a good model to work from; if not, here is my method to make downsizing as easy as possible:

I gave every room or space a name that I wrote on a piece of paper with columns labeled "Give Away," "Throw," "Stay," and "Move." That helped me not to forget anything when different organizations (the old people's association, the Red Cross, etc.) came to collect things.

When my house was sold, it turned out that the new owners wanted to buy and keep some of the furniture. I placed this furniture in the "Stay" column and also stickered each piece with a label marked "Stay" in red.

A little later I was able to find a two-room apartment in a different town that I knew well from an earlier time in my life, one in which two of my children lived and where I still had a few friends.

I did not plan to pack, carry, and move myself. Now it was time to get written estimates from at least two different movers, but before I decided on a moving company, I wanted to do more preparation.

MAPPING OUT YOUR NEW SPACE

Before I hired the movers, I went to my new dwelling and carefully measured every space. The floor plan of an apartment that the broker provides you with seldom gives the exact measurements, and it is so important that they really are exact. Imagine that the movers have carried a big chest of drawers up the stairs and it is two inches too wide. That would really be a waste of time and very annoying for both you and the movers.

So first I bought a large pad of graph paper and outlined

the floor plan of the apartment on it. I also measured all the furniture that I hoped would fit in my reduced space and drew them like squares and rectangles on a piece of the graph paper. I named them all so that I knew what they represented and then cut each of them out.

Then it was easy to furnish my new rooms by pushing around all the squares and rectangles of paper in the floorplan I had outlined. There was of course not room for all the paper furniture I had cut out, but the most important thing was to figure out which of the things that I planned to bring would actually have a chance to find a nice place in my new home.

Any items that didn't fit went through the same procedure as all the other things I had gotten rid of previously. I asked my children first, then the auctioneer, then friends and neighbors, etc.

The day before the move, I made sure for the last time that all the things that were going to stay were properly marked so the movers didn't bring things I had already decided I did not need and that would not fit. This was as important as changing my postal address and switching my water meter and electricity bills to the new owner's name.

Moving into the new place was easy since I already knew where all the things would fit. I felt very happy and content that I did not have to ask for help later on to move things around once I had settled in.

HOME

I moved from the west coast of Sweden to Stockholm ten years ago. I made the right decision not to hurry when I moved out of my house. I took my time to plan my move and to really think over how I wanted my future to be.

This new apartment building has a lovely inner yard with a lot of greenery, trees, and flowers. There is an outdoor seating area, a children's playground, bicycle stands, a garage for those who need one, a guest apartment that one can rent for a modest price for a couple of days, a well-equipped laundry room, and good access to public transportation. It is important to look for the amenities that matter to you before you buy or rent a new place to live in.

I don't think I will ever move again, but since I am now between eighty and one hundred, I do not think it will do harm to make a new inventory of all that I have. I own too many clothes and too many books and I do not need sixteen plates when there is only room for six around my table. Also, I am sure that the number of tablecloths and napkins can be reduced.

I have bought a small and easy-to-use paper shredder. I am looking forward to going through old letters and other papers that are no longer important—papers from a business my husband and I once ran, papers from other financial and banking transactions, and a lot of paid invoices with receipts attached with staples. If there is one thing I have learned from death cleaning, it is that I hate staples.

My husband was very orderly, which was nice at the time, but today the staples are a problem. I have to remove these nasty little metal pieces, one by one, so that they do not destroy my precious shredder. Tape would have made my life easier today. Keep this in mind when stapling papers together.

A FEW THOUGHTS ON ACCUMULATION

I have spent my life painting pictures. Luckily, a big part of being an artist is being able to part with the stuff you paint. I have sold or given away my life's work, gradually, at the same pace as I have produced it. When I had to downsize my lifestyle, I had a number of paintings that I wasn't satisfied with. I had saved them because I wanted to improve them. In my new home there was no room for these paintings, so I got rid of them. I threw them on the fire.

Maybe the fact that I have gotten rid of my artwork all my life makes me unsentimental about getting rid of other things, too.

It is amazing, and also a little strange, how many things we accumulate in a lifetime.

Things

New modern appliances such as deluxe coffee makers, high-speed mixers, and sci-fi pots and pans fill our kitchens, while we still keep the old coffee brewer, whisk, and skillets. In the bathroom you might have ten years of the latest eyeshadows, or all the nail polishes of the last seasons. Medicine cabinets are often full of trendy vitamins that no one takes and medicines that have expired. Even tablecloths and bed linens have a fashion. We get new ones all the time, even if the old ones are not yet worn out.

We feel like last year's colonial style of dark wood and bamboo has to be exchanged for this year's clean white

Nordic minimalism, with straight lines and no fuss. If not, we seem to think that it is impossible to live in our homes. This is wasteful but not a huge problem if we remember to get rid of last year's things before we buy the new ones.

This cycle of consumption we are all part of will eventually destroy our planet—but it doesn't have to destroy the relationship you have with whomever you leave behind.

When you live in a big city where people seem to replace their kitchen and bathroom fixtures as often as I replace an old sweater, you will see huge Dumpsters on the sidewalks filled with bathtubs, sinks, toilets. When the next owner wants to put their personal stamp on the apartment, everything is changed again; it may be in one year or two!

When you are between eighty and one hundred, you do not know many people your age who want or have the energy to do such large-scale renovations or care about putting their stamp on things in this way. That is another benefit of death cleaning: thinking more about how to reuse, recycle, and make your life simpler and a bit (or a lot) smaller. Living smaller is a relief.

Clothes

When you get older, your lifestyle changes, as does your need for certain garments. I am sure you will gladly sell or give away gear that is more suitable for downhill skiing, ballet, or perhaps scuba diving when you realize you are not likely to use them again.

I have gone skiing in a bikini on a wonderful, sunny winter day. It is strange to think that a swimsuit would work in the Alps, when ski boots most certainly don't work when swimming. So what do you keep when you get old? The swimsuit, of course.

People of all ages buy lots of outfits. Not because we need to, but because it makes us happy for a while. We feel better, more attractive, and we love the thought that the new outfit suits us perfectly!

Men my age do not really have the problem of too many outfits. They wear more of a uniform. But young men today seem more interested in clothing and fashion. So eventually they, too, will have the same problems cleaning out their wardrobes as we women have today.

I have noticed that no one seems to mend anything these days, and the most expensive trousers are the ones that come with holes and patches. Perhaps it *is* time for new generations to learn how to sew and to fix things, as it would help our planet. Secondhand boutiques are popping up everywhere. That is wonderful! It's even called "vintage" now. But what do you say when one of your guests shows up in your old dress? I really have to get used to that thought and have not yet figured out how to handle such a situation should it happen to me one day.

I was recently at a party with young people. A woman walked in with a very nice dress. I complimented her on it and she was so proud that it was secondhand—almost as if it had been Dior. So maybe society is changing. There is hope for the planet after all!

A Note on Children's Clothes

When my sister and I were children long ago, we had a seamstress, as was the custom at that time. Her job was to resize and sometimes update our clothes. Mrs. Andersson arrived early in the morning to take our measurements before we went to school. She worked in our home for a few days each season.

I sewed a lot for my own children, and I have not forgotten all the trouser bottoms that I mended in the wintertime if my children could not find some cardboard to sit on when sledding downhill.

Sometimes it is very hard to give away children's clothes. For me it is because they are so small and cute and it is such fun to show a tiny shirt to a young man who is now almost six feet tall and say, "This was yours."

Later, when that six-foot-tall young man becomes a father, it can be nice for him to see his child in something that he once wore. The children's clothing of yesterday was of better quality than today. I remember how my mother made baby clothes for my children. She sewed them out of the same soft material that handkerchiefs were made of, and had all the seams on the outside so as not to scratch the baby's skin. I kept some of these items in a box in the attic, in case I was to be blessed with grandchildren. And when grandchildren failed to arrive, I would take the box down and remind my lazy children of what I wanted. It worked. I now have eight grandchildren. And no baby clothes in the attic.

But if smaller family members don't need them, the best thing is of course to give them to charity.

Books

In our family we have always liked to read and keep books. A Christmas without a book for a present is a disappointment.

Books are generally hard to sell. I suggest that you let family and friends browse among the books you can live without and take what they want. Sometimes books have notes in the margins, written by people you know. These books can be difficult to get rid of for sentimental reasons. I suggest you give the book and notes one last read before you pass it on. When buying used books, I often look for volumes with notes in the margins written by strangers. It gives the book some extra character. So don't be afraid of giving away books with notes in them.

If you have several books on a specific subject, such as art, gardening, cooking, science, or, as I had, nautical books, you might find someone who is interested in buying the lot.

In addition to books to read and enjoy, most Swedish families kept an encyclopedia set on the bookshelf. Nowadays with the Internet, I did not feel that I had a need or enough space for my encyclopedia in my new apartment. So, when I moved from my house, I called the nearby school and they were glad to take care of these twenty-eight (I think) big, heavy books. It made me so happy that I gave them a bookcase as well.

I only keep books that I still haven't read or books that I keep returning to. In my case, these are mostly books about art and some reference books, such as a dictionary, a thesaurus, and an atlas.

When I was death cleaning my house before my move, my greatest problem with my books were the Bibles. I called the local church, but they did not want any more Bibles, not even old ones in leather bindings. They did not have any ideas for what I should do with them. I kept two—someone had written on the inside covers the birth and death dates of people from my and my husband's families who had lived long ago. The others I had to throw away. I do not know why I felt so bad about it. I guess that these Bibles had meant a lot to people who were in some way related to me, even if I had never met them. They were cherished at a time when books really meant something to their owners—long before Harry Potter and other bestsellers were invented.

Here in Stockholm on the 14th of August is a big annual book sale. A whole long street in the center of the city is occupied by tables with books that people want to sell. It is a fantastic day for those who want to get rid of some books and for those who want to pick up more. If there is not something like this where you live, maybe you can help start one.

THE KITCHEN

One of my daughters has a sign in her kitchen that reads, "I kiss better than I cook!" It is an informative and fair warning to her guests—that they might well have an evening of all sorts of surprises, perhaps both good and bad, ahead of them. I like to cook, although I'm certainly not a star chef, but I have collected many kitchen utensils during my life that I now must figure out what to do with.

When we lived in Asia, I bought utensils that were practical, beautiful, and unlike anything I had seen before. Porcelain spoons, for example, so good to eat hot soup with, as one doesn't burn one's lips. A few large ladles made of coconut shells, great for soups, stews, and salads. I also have a small tea strainer of plaited bamboo, far too brittle and beautiful for daily use, but so well crafted. After more than twenty years they still look just as pretty. These small things will be easy to place with anyone.

But I also had my big wok! Made of very thin sheet metal, black as sin, it is lovely to fry and boil with, especially when cooking Asian food. A wok like this must be handled like a baby, cleaned and dried thoroughly after each use and sometimes, especially if the climate is humid, greased with a little oil so as not to rust.

Once I was invited to a tea party in Singapore. Everyone had to wear a hat—it was compulsory! I had not worn a hat for twenty years or so, and was not really well stocked in that area. I didn't know what to do.

And then I saw my wok hanging on a nail above our gas stove. I put it on my head, taped an orchid on the front brim as decoration, and tied it under my chin with coarse household string. Believe it or not, I won first prize and received a beautiful glass bottle of Schiaparelli's perfume Shocking for my efforts. Wow!

A son and his family willingly took the wok off my hands. They love to cook, and the food made in this wok, I imagine, has a special flavor. Moreover, they have a gas stove and also the option to use the wok as it is meant to be used, over an open fire, and in their case outdoors.

Knowing that they had the right conditions to use this precious wok made it easy for me to place it with them. Thinking of the new home in which your object will find itself is very important as you do your job. Don't offer things that do not fit the recipient's taste or the space in which they live. It will be a burden to them, and if they think your feelings might be hurt, it may be difficult for them to say "No, thank you."

If you are not selling something or giving it to charity, or throwing it away, careful thought in deciding on a new perfect home for it will satisfy both you and the recipient. To know something will be well used and have a new home is a joy.

When death cleaning your servingware, there are two scenarios: either you are moving to a smaller home, in which case you need to consider the storage space available there, or you are staying put but have more plates, glasses, mugs, forks, etc., than you can use.

If you still entertain guests, I would suggest keeping one set of dishes that match the number of guests you can fit at your table. The same goes for knives, forks, glasses, and cups. If you want to decorate your table, use flowers or bright paper napkins instead of multiple plates and cloth napkins in every shade and color.

I have kept, and still use, some special china plates from

Japan, which I will give to my children. Simpler plates and surplus glasses have been given to charity.

Cookbooks and Family Recipes

When my kitchen was larger than it is today, I had a bookshelf reserved for cookbooks. Nowadays I mostly use the Internet when I search for a recipe. I type the name of the dish I want to cook into Google and suddenly I get several possibilities, each with an image more alluring than the one before. Amazing!

These days I now have only two real cookbooks left. By "real," I mean books you can hold, browse, and ponder as you search for something to make. One of the books I more or less made myself over the years; it is full of recipes that I was given by friends and relatives or had cut out of newspapers. Most of these recipes I have been slowly throwing away, the time-consuming ones and ones for cakes and cookies. I no longer enjoy standing in the kitchen for hours and I am not much of a cookie monster and don't really like them—though the children certainly loved them.

Some real gems remain, though, such as my mother's meat loaf, my mother-in-law's best *gaffelkakor* (a type of shortbread cookie topped with the imprint of a fork), my old neighbor Andréa's rosehip marmalade, and a few more favorites that may be of interest to someone else, either because they are so good, or because they are recipes that are not easy to find, or because they have resonant memories to them that my loved ones may want to conjure up in their own kitchens.

Three of the recipes I have saved are ones I found in my father's kitchen drawer many years ago. The recipes were handwritten neatly by the cook who lived with us when I was a small child. She was very kind, and I remember that I was allowed to sit in the kitchen and watch as she baked. She used to give me treats of raisins, perhaps to keep me quiet, even if only for a moment. Her three recipes are for pickles, deep-fried herring, and french steaks. Every other recipe she cooked was stored safely in her head.

The second cookbook I have saved comes from Singapore, where we lived for six years and where I and many friends gathered recipes for a cookbook that we created and sold for charity. My tattered copy is full of delightful recipes donated by women—and one man—from all over the world. There is ceviche from South America, lamb curry from Malaysia, cake from the Swedish province of Värmland, and directions for how to make a perfect Singapore Sling. (Personally, I think that drink tastes like someone cleaned out the pantry to find the ingredients—but I guess it fits in well with the wide-ranging tastes in the book!)

And there are cookies from Mexico, rye bread from the former Czechoslovakia, and much more. Many of the recipe donors often hosted guests and were obviously very proud to offer something that represented their part of the world. Thus, the amazing wealth of recipes. Browsing the book still takes me on a global tour of tastes and a wander through memories of the many fascinating people I knew at that time in my life.

When we came home again, to the Swedish coastal province of Bohuslän, where I am from, I thought about collecting old recipes that local women cherished and kept hidden somewhere—good things to cook that used local ingredients and recipes that may have been handed down, perhaps for generations. Now I do not think I have the time to do this, but maybe someone else who reads this will take the hint and get started. Now! Time is of the essence; these women might be older than I am.

I find it has been easy to get rid of printed cookbooks, no matter how helpful they have been through the years. It is the personal recipes and stories that I most want to keep and continue to savor.

My next-door neighbor for a few years in Bohuslän was named Andréa. She was the very capable widow of a fisherman. She was a good, dear friend. I painted a picture of her once that represented a flowering dogwood tree. It is reminiscent of a magnolia tree but larger and covered with dense flowers. Strong and beautiful. Just as Andréa was. She had many wonderful recipes and a few I would like to share with you: pickled rosehip marmalade, sherry made from red beets, and classic cheesecake Bohuslän-style (see the Appendix on page 109 for the recipes).

One afternoon, Andréa invited me over to sample her red beet sherry. It had a beautiful amber color and tasted really smooth and warm and wonderful. That day she told me about the custom of fishermen's widows. She said that every morning, after her husband had died, she would take the leftover porridge and place it where his fishing boat had been moored. In no time at all a gull would fly in and dine on what she had provided. She said the bird was the spirit of her deceased husband. I always think of this when I see a seagull.

My own husband was buried on a glorious early summer day. Small girls, his grandchildren, were so serious in their bright dresses. The boys climbed up and balanced on a low cemetery wall. Someone read a poem by Frans G. Bengtsson, a Swedish author and poet whom my husband liked very much. The poem, "A Gazelle," ends in the following way:

The seagull knows a way to rest.
The human heart, on earth, does not know yet.

On the gravel path close to my husband's grave, a young seagull walked slowly past. I could not help but smile.

THINGS, THINGS, AND MORE THINGS

Beautiful things such as an African wooden bird, strange things like a singing magnetic pig, and funny things like a solar-powered waving bear are all things that I adore. My vice is really things. It took me a while to understand this, but you can enjoy all these things without owning them. Even though this may sometimes seem quite hard to do, training yourself to enjoy only looking at things, instead of buying them, is very nice and also a good practice. You *really* can't take everything with you, so maybe it is better to not try to own it all.

All the things I mentioned above are small and easy to give away. If you are invited to lunch, don't buy the host flowers or a new present—give her one of your things.

When I browse through an interior-decorating magazine, I sometimes get so tired! Many of these homes look as if all the furniture was supplied by the same store. Colorless, plain, perfect, and without any charm at all. Too many pieces for decoration arranged on parade or in strange, affected compositions. Who will want to dust them, I wonder.

But there are many homes that have a lot to teach. Beautiful, practical, and sparsely furnished. Truly inspiring homes that are easy to keep clean. I still try to learn from these rooms. I reflect and maybe rethink my own living space, and then probably will get rid of a few more things!

IF IT WAS YOUR SECRET, THEN KEEP IT THAT WAY (OR HOW TO DEATH CLEAN HIDDEN, DANGEROUS, AND SECRET THINGS)

In connection with my father's relocation, there were a few things that worried him. He was a medical doctor and he kept all his patients' case books in his office. Of course he needed to get rid of them in a safe manner. Everything was written by hand or on his little Remington typewriter. Computers were not invented yet. Because of that it was easy to get rid of his files without a trace. We burned all the papers in an old oil drum at our country house.

Another problem was a parcel at the very back of his desk drawer. It contained a large piece of arsenic! It had been there for almost thirty years, since the time we were worried that the Germans would invade our country. Why my father had kept it there for so long was hard to understand. Maybe he had just forgotten it. Maybe he thought it would not hurt to have some poison available. The pharmacist looked a bit puzzled when I handed over the block of arsenic, but he took care of it.

While cleaning out my parents' house, one thing puzzled me, though. My mother had a huge cabinet for linen. Freshly pressed towels and napkins were put at the bottom of the piles so that the rotation of all the things was even. At the very back behind pleated pillowcase ribbons, I found her vice. Several cartons of cigarettes.

What are vices? I guess habits that are not so good for us. We've now become dependent on our cell phones, games, and many other things that—unlike cigarette cartons—do not reveal themselves after we are dead.

But there are people who have wardrobes filled with empty gin and whiskey bottles that they have secretly finished off. And there are many other things that people love to gossip about after someone's death.

Maybe Grandfather had ladies' underwear in his drawer and maybe Grandma had a dildo in hers. But what does that matter now? They are no longer among us; if we liked them, it really should be nothing for us to worry about. Let us each have our small preferences, as long as nobody gets hurt.

But it is perhaps a nice gift to those loved ones who may be death cleaning for us later if we do a little bit of our own cleaning now—to reduce these types of belongings a bit before we leave our present life.

Save your favorite dildo—but throw away the other fifteen!

There's no sense in saving things that will shock or upset your family after you are gone.

Perhaps you have saved letters, documents, or diaries that contain information or family stories you would never wish to embarrass your descendants with. While we seem to live in a culture where everyone thinks they have the right to every secret, I do not agree. If you think the secret will cause your loved ones harm or unhappiness, then make sure to destroy them. Make a bonfire or shove them into the hungry shredder.

THE PERILS OF MAN CAVES

Another space that seemed like it could be time-consuming to go through was my husband's toolshed. If you own a house, it is very convenient to have someone who also lives there who can be a combination of carpenter, painter, plumber, and general repairer of things.

This can be especially so if you live far from a major city where all these professionals seem to locate their businesses. It can be very expensive if you need to call for technical assistance all the time if you live in an out-of-the-way place, as we did for many years.

Bicycles, boats, and garden paraphernalia all need various tools and repairing to keep them functioning. There are endless reasons to justify the purchase of new tools, and men—or at least those in my generation and the generations before mine—seem to jump at any chance to visit the hardware store!

But let's be truthful: you don't need to live in a house to have an overload of tools. One of my children, who lives in a small rental apartment in a city, has a closet full of odd nuts, bolts, screws, bent nails, and fixtures that he thinks he might need one day. He hasn't opened that closet for years.

After all the children (who also need special tools: our children liked to build huts, rafts, and tiny boxcars—we call them *lådbil* in Sweden) had left home, my husband continued to organize and examine his many tools every day.

His *snickarbod* (Swedish for "toolshed") gradually became what I believe today is called a "man cave." In

Swedish we also now sometimes call it *mansdagis*—a male kindergarten, which makes me smile and which feels like an entirely appropriate word.

Have you noticed that many people find more pleasure in organizing their stuff than in actually using their stuff? I have, and I admire that spirit of order immensely.

As I investigated my husband's *snickarbod*, I saw that everything was so beautifully in order: chisel, level, rotary hammers, pliers and hacksaw frames, and lots of screws and nails! Pumps and rubber valves, special oils for the bikes. It sounds almost erotic! The mower also needed special oils and grindstones and the boat required all sorts of sandpaper, paint, and other gadgets. All these things had been carefully and lovingly organized by my husband.

There were a few boxes marked with their more loosely organized contents but most of his tools were hung on the wall, matched to carefully drawn outlines to show where they belonged and as a reminder in case someone borrowed something and failed to return it to the right place. A master of order, my husband was.

If I had entertained any thoughts about becoming a craftsman, my husband's toolshed should have been an inspiration. I could have started sculpting in rock, iron, concrete; built wooden projects; connected engines for some unusual invention. Everything I could need was all there, with warranties and instructions beautifully organized in binders.

But these were not my ambitions and were not how I thought I would be spending my time.

Instead I picked out one hammer, some pliers, a selection of screwdrivers, and a yardstick for the small repairs and adjustments I thought I could accomplish myself. Hanging up paintings and shelves, and putting up hooks for towels or garments isn't too difficult when you have the right tools. Even if you are very old. My children took some of the other tools, and their friends were happy to help clean out the rest as tools are relatively expensive in Sweden.

I found that it was especially efficient to invite young men over to choose things for themselves. They were starting their own man caves, and my husband's *snickarbod* was empty in no time.

To empty the *snickarbod* was, in the end, fairly easy, both practically and emotionally. For me there was no connection to the items, apart from the fact that they had belonged to my husband. I had many other things of his that I felt more emotionally connected to. I never had to stop my cleaning to reminisce over an object and slow down my work. In the case of a man trying to death clean his toolshed . . . well, that could take years, and I don't feel I have much knowledge to offer on how to do that.

UNWANTED THINGS

If you receive things you don't really want from your parents or someone else who wants to reduce the number of their possessions in their home, you should be honest and say, "No, thank you, I don't have room for this." Just moving things someone does not want in their house to your house is not a good solution for anyone.

Or you can do as I have done when I have received things that I did not really like. For a while, I put the object a little bit out of the way so that when the giver comes to visit they can see the object and feel happy about having given it a new home in my house. When I get bored of the object, I'll get rid of it—either to a charity, or to someone who admires it more than I do. But you never know—I have kept a few things that I did not originally like and they have become treasures to me; sometimes our tastes mature.

If I give a present to someone, I understand that it may not stay with that person forever. Do any of us really keep track of everything we give away? I don't. Things break. Even a popcorn machine does not work for eternity. I will never feel guilty for not keeping presents forever. To be grateful and happy for a present when you first receive it is something different, because that gratitude is not connected to the thing itself but to the giver who gave it to you.

I do know people who maintain what we in Sweden call a *fulskåp*, a cabinet for the ugly.

A *fulskåp* is a cupboard full of gifts you can't stand to look at, and which are impossible to regift. Usually these are presents from distant aunts and uncles that you put on display when the giver comes to visit.

This is a bad idea. If aunts and uncles see their gifts on show, they will only give you more! And who can keep track of who gave what to whom and when? If you don't like something, get rid of it.

COLLECTIONS, COLLECTORS, AND HOARDERS

Have we not always collected things? Sticks and logs for the fire, berries and roots to eat? But collecting things just for fun is entirely different. I remember collecting shells on a beach of the Swedish west coast where I was born. I still have some of them in a bowl together with some from more exotic places. Beautiful to look at, nice to hold in your hand. When I was a child we collected badges, bottle caps, matchboxes, and pictures of football players and movie stars. Also I remember collecting the nice tissue papers that oranges were wrapped in when they were imported again after the war in the forties. We had not seen bananas or oranges for many, many years.

We also collected bookmarks, which we traded with classmates and other children during breaks. I had a very big and beautiful bookmark that I offered to a boy in my class if he kissed me. I think I did that to try to impress my best friend, who was four years older and was always bragging about how many boys had kissed her. But my appointed kisser never kissed me, so my lovely bookmark stayed with me, and I think I was just as happy about that.

Later I became more serious about collecting. Stamps became a quite lucrative and also instructive hobby for those who made an effort.

I had an interesting neighbor many years ago. He used the basement of his villa as a shelter for all sorts of things. Flat tires, a sled, a playpen for children, and other things. Over the years the storage became quite full. The lady of the house discovered that there was a back door on the other side that led to the same space. Now and then she grabbed a few things and took them to the dump. When her husband wanted to squeeze in more stuff, he consequently succeeded.

This summer I met a lady selling things at a local junk market. She and her husband were going to move, and when she went through the drawers in her kitchen she realized among other things that they had twelve cheese slicers. She was not a collector, just a bit careless. Then I read about a guy who collected eggcups. He was a real collector and had one thousand cups from different factories all over the world. Just eggcups. Amazing!

I had a beloved nanny. She collected coffee cups with saucers. She married a Lutheran priest and loved to offer church coffee in all her cups after Sunday mass in their parish. Sometimes large collections can be useful, but sometimes they can become a burden for you and later for your family.

If you want to get rid of a collection of your own, and your family doesn't seem to want it, I think the best way is to contact an auction house and listen to what they say. If they do not show any interest, you might find a buyer on the Internet.

A genuine collector enjoys collecting specific categories of things and has good systems for keeping track of the items in the collection, and looks for items that are missing in the collection. The collection will make other people happy, too. Think of museums. Are they not the results of industrious collectors?

But people who just hoard things and papers without

meaning or purpose may actually be affected by an illness. These people can fill rooms in their home with so many things that it is impossible to enter them at all. In some families and intimate relationships, hoarding can become a big problem. Unfortunately, I do not have much helpful advice for you in this situation. This hoarding disease can be treated. But if a doctor cannot help, the only thing I can think to do is order a big container when the time comes.

IN THE GARDEN

Most people have a hobby, something we like to do every day. Hopefully we are lucky enough to do it as a profession, but otherwise at least we can always do it in our spare time.

I loved the garden I had at my old house. For me it was joyous to go out into the greenery, to look and become absorbed. I would spend hours occupied by pruning, dividing, pulling weeds, replanting, or just being pleased by a plant that had recently opened a lovely flower. A garden is always full of adventure and expectation.

Later in the summertime I could fill a bowl with raspberries, give a sun-warmed tomato or a whole cucumber each to my grandchildren. These joyful moments will unfortunately disappear when you move up some floors, as I have.

When I still had my garden, I had many tools to take care of it with. I kept all my rakes and spades in my *redskapsbod* (Swedish for "gardening shed"). As I was moving to a place with no garden I let the tools in the shed stay with the new owners of our house. They were happy to have such nice equipment and I was glad to give them to people who were anxious to keep my garden pretty and alive.

If you are lucky to have a balcony or even some window boxes or a sunny windowsill, you can still have some perennials. I have an ivy plant and some honeysuckle and they survive in their pots year after year without any winter cover even in this cold Nordic climate, where last November we only had a few precious hours of direct sunlight. Every spring when there is no longer a risk of night frost, I add some summer flowers such as petunias, forget-me-nots, or violets, and herbs like basil, thyme, chives, and parsley to my tiny balcony garden.

In my apartment building, we have a garden group. The members take care of the vegetation in our yard. Everyone who loves gardening can get their fair share there.

In addition to green hedges and some flowering bushes, there are cherry trees that bloom so nicely in springtime and later on offer sweet berries. In the building's yard, we have perennials that always have some plants in bloom. There is rhubarb and there are also herbs and spices like sage, thyme, rosemary, chives, and lemon balm. Anyone from the garden group or from the building can pick some for cooking, or even just to smell.

The best thing about this kind of cooperative garden is that new members will join every year. So if one day you feel that you do not have the strength to work in the yard, the other members will take care of the vegetation and you do not have to feel bad about that. Could it be better?

When I think of everything that grows and when I think of everything that we shred, tear, and break to pieces and even bury to get rid of, it is a good thing that all that junk does not come back bigger and stronger the next year in the way that some plants and weeds do.

PETS

And what do you do with your pets when you move from one home to another, or even from one country to another, and must plan for your future?

Mice, guinea pigs, hamsters, cats, dogs, birds, and fish were all animals that we kept over the years in our family. It sounds like a zoo, but we didn't have all of these creatures simultaneously.

Hampus, the guinea pig, belonged to one of my sons. When he was about eight years old, he let Hampus out of his cage and put him on our dining table, just when dinner was finishing. Grandma was visiting and I had picked a large bouquet of goldenrod flowers, which I'd placed in a vase in the middle of the table to brighten up the room.

Hampus approached the flowers carefully, sniffed them, and then proceeded to eat several of the blooms. Shortly thereafter and quite suddenly the little guinea pig gave a violent twitch, flipped onto his back, and lay very still. Hampus was dead.

This was of course very sad. My son sobbed, looked at his grandmother, and said:

"When you die, Grandmother, I will be as sad as I am now when Hampus has died."

His grandmother, being a very wise old woman, understood that he was honoring her with his somewhat shocking statement. She took him into her lap and let him stay there the whole evening, comforting him.

When we moved from the United States back to Sweden in the mid-seventies, we had to leave two of our dogs behind with two different families. At that time, there was a four-month quarantine for animals coming to Sweden from the United States. Quarantine is a cold and lonely place, and something we did not wish for our tiny friends.

We thought a lot about how a little dog might respond when the safe home it has grown accustomed to is suddenly taken away and it must face a new environment— we wanted to find a place that was just as safe. I contacted a kennel that bred Norfolk terriers. It was not many miles from our house and was run by a nice middle-aged woman who said we were welcome to drop by.

The kennel was well maintained, clean, and full of happy little doggies of different ages. The woman knew of our worries about having to place our dog, Duffy, with a new family. She walked us around the grounds and let us meet many dogs. Then we sat down for a chat. While we chatted, a small doggy sat down very close to my son. The woman laughed and said to my boy: "You see, that dog doesn't know you, and still he would gladly go home with you!" We sighed with relief, felt reassured, and were glad to have made the trip.

A secretary from the office where my husband worked took care of the little Norfolk terrier, so he ended up in a good home where he was loved. I even got a comforting letter from Duffy's new mistress who told me that all was well.

Kennels usually have many contacts with people who are waiting to buy a puppy or an older dog. Our basset hound also got a good home through the kennel. What a nice, funny, and crazy dog he was. He loved to lie down in all the well-kept, pretty flowerbeds of the neighborhood and to steal sandwiches and other edibles if given the opportunity. He had a good life with his new family, but as to the fate of their garden, I never found out.

Once you get used to having pets around, life can feel terribly empty without them. One day in Singapore, one of my sons and I set off to the SPCA (the Society for the Prevention of Cruelty to Animals), where all kinds of abandoned animals were taken care of by full-time staff.

When we came home that afternoon, it was in the company of a new family member: Taxes, a large, sandy-brown, old, and rather tired Great Dane. Taxes soon made his home on a thick blanket on our terrace. He slept a lot, and most of the time slept so deeply that—even though he looked very fearsome, he was so kindhearted—he once let some robbers step right over him without even trying to stop them when we were out of town.

Taxes was so old that he had a graying beard; he was also rheumatic and could only eat a vegetarian diet of brown rice mixed with egg and boiled vegetables. The mixture was so tasty I often caught my teenagers eating the dog food as a snack when they came home from school.

Despite these human competitors for his food, Taxes got a big bowl of vegetarian delight out on the balcony every afternoon. At every one of his mealtimes, two big, black jackdaw birds would perch on the railing nearby to watch him. They sat there in silence, blinked their eyes, and nodded their heads. Taxes always left a couple of morsels of his food in the bowl. Then he went to his blanket to digest, and immediately the jackdaws would come swooping down, land gently, and eat the leftovers. Every day! It was quite charming.

To own a dog is very nice, but it is also a big responsibility. If you get sick or have to move and cannot take care of your beloved friend for a while or permanently, you have to make sure that your good companion gets the best care and friendship possible. Most dogs are social and can easily make new human contacts, and they will enjoy their life without you. But with our dog Taxes, it was different since he was so old and was often in physical pain.

When we had to go back to Sweden for good, I didn't know what to do. I could not imagine leaving Taxes to an unknown fate. He was too kind to start anew and too old for me to find a family to take him in. I did not think he would be likely to survive the four months of cold quarantine it would take to get him to Sweden.

Finally, I consulted with our vet and made the only decision that I felt I could; it was terrible and difficult to make. When they gave him the injection, Taxes sank quietly and heavily in my arms. It was so very sad, but it was the only option that we could see.

To let things, people, and pets go when there is no better alternative is a lesson that has been very difficult for me to learn and a lesson that life, as it goes further along, is teaching me more and more often.

If I were to have a pet now when I am this old, I would like that pet to be old, too. I am too lazy to raise a puppy, and can't go for the long walks a young dog requires. If I were to get a dog, and I think about doing this sometimes, I would go to a kennel and ask if they had an old and tired doggy that

I could take care of. You could do the same, if your favorite pet dies and you still want an animal companion.

Should your pet live longer than you, then you might be creating a problem for those around you. Talk to your family and neighbors before you get yourself an old lazy dog. Would they be willing to take care of the animal when you are not able to? If not, you should reconsider getting an animal at all.

The Story of Klumpeduns

Is this a book about animals, you might be wondering. It is not. If it were, I would have to tell you all the crazy stories about our fish, our many birds, and all our lovely cats: Mien, Little Cat, Little Fur, Shreds. But there is one cat I do want to tell you about: Klumpeduns (the Swedish word for a clumsy person).

One day, a big, light-red-colored cat appeared in our home. My husband never had anything against cats, but he had never wished for one. Nevertheless, that red cat immediately adopted my husband and wanted to be close to him whenever he could. We named him Klumpeduns because he—unlike most cats—was always bumping into things and breaking them, leaping for things and missing them, or would just as suddenly fall off the chair he was sitting on.

Every night when the sports news was on TV and my husband sat in his spacious armchair enjoying it, Klumpeduns would come padding along, leap up, and make himself comfortable on the arm of the chair.

Later, when my husband had to move to a nursing home, the cat mourned and missed him, but every night he would still jump up (if he didn't miss!) and lie on the arm of the chair, even though I seldom watched the sports news.

One day the nursing home called and told me that my husband had suddenly died. I had visited him in the morning and although he had been quite sick, it was still a shock. How could it not be? The nursing home people asked if I could come and fetch his clothes and other belongings, as they needed the room immediately.

I of course had many other things to sort out once I got to the nursing home, but I brought everything from his room back to our home. I put all his clothes in a pile just inside the front door, too tired to take care of it all just then. Some friends had invited me to come visit, and I really needed some companionship, so I left.

When I came home, Klumpeduns lay stretched out and sad on the pile of my husband's clothes. I cried.

I had cried so much during the many years that my husband had been drifting away from me. That evening, all my sorrows found their focus on that cat. I suddenly felt very guilty at having left the poor creature alone with his grief. Klumpeduns himself died in the months after.

Not that I really believe in an afterlife, but sometimes I find myself imagining that Klumpeduns has found a comfortable armrest and his good old friend in some other distant place.

AT LAST: PHOTOGRAPHS

I reached the stage in my death cleaning where I had to consider all my photos. They can be really hard to deal with! On many levels.

First, going through photographs is quite sentimental. So many memories come back, memories you will want to keep. Maybe to give to your family. But remember, your memories and your family's are not always the same.

What one family member might think is worth saving another might find completely uninteresting. If you have several children, do not ever believe that they will behave or think in the same way. No, no, not at all.

Even though we can all now save lots of photographs on our computers, I believe that most people still prefer to look at them in an album. While growing up, each of our children had an album of their own; since we took a lot of photographs, it was always exciting when new film was developed and the packet of photographs arrived in the mailbox. Every child decided which photos they wanted and they put their name or mark on the back side of the photo so that we knew which ones to order copies for. Within a few days, the photos arrived and were put in each child's album. They each still have their album.

If you want to buy a nice album, there are many kinds to choose from. I prefer albums with loose-leaf systems so that you can increase the number of pages as the album grows and time goes by.

Sure, it is nice to sit with someone like-minded and browse through a photo album. You can point and talk about when such and such event happened and perhaps also about the one who held the camera. That is like the back side of the picture that you cannot see.

One of my daughters-in-law told me about a little girl in the nursery where she works. She wanted to draw her best friend. When the drawing was finished, the little girl turned over the paper to draw the back of her friend on the reverse side. What a wonderful idea.

So what should you keep in mind when cleaning out your photographs?

Before I put any in an album, I usually discard multiple photos at once, simply because they are bad or because you or other people look completely crazy.

I have also always liked to be able to name everyone in a

picture. Now that I am the oldest person in my family, if I don't know the names of the people in the photos, nobody else in the family is likely to. More work for the shredder.

But sometimes I hesitate. Really old photos may well have a historical and cultural value even without knowing the names of the people in the photos: to look at the clothes, the cars, and life in a street only thirty to forty years ago can be really fun. So maybe I should be a little cautious and show a few samples to my children to understand what they think is interesting and whether it is something they would like me to save for them.

My father loved to take pictures, and he was a very good photographer. I have taken many photos during the years, and three of the children are very talented photographers. As a result, we have too many photos in our family, and it really is my fault and therefore it is me who has to do the cleaning up. Me and my hungry shredder.

One problem with my photos was the huge amount of slides that I have, all kept in cassettes. One cassette can hold up to eighty slides, and I had many of them. We used to look at the slides projected on the wall. That was a nice entertainment since we just had one TV channel fifty years ago and children's programs were rare. I think *Scooby-Doo* was shown only once a week.

One autumn a couple of years ago I decided to do

something about the slides. I bought a little film scanner and spent most of my spare time going through them, pictures from when my oldest son was born and the following twenty-five years.

With the help of the scanner, I moved all the pictures I wanted to share to my computer and then exported them to a USB memory stick for each child. It is really amazing how much a little USB memory stick—not even two inches long—can hold.

I was happy to have Christmas presents that year. I just put them in envelopes and sent them through the post.

When you have lived a long life, it is so easy to get lost among memories from a long time ago. That will take a lot of time, I know. It will be much nicer to go through old photos in the peace and quiet later on after you have made some successful progress on other categories of objects and things. Plus, photos don't take up too much space and this is not a task your children will really resent being left to handle. They might even enjoy it.

I remember one time when all my grown-up children, some with families, visited to celebrate a birthday. I had pulled together a lot of photos and sorted them into envelopes marked with the children's names. We were all gathered around our dinner table.

At first, things were quiet as people opened their envelopes and began to look through their photos, but after a while I heard them chatter: "Wow! Look at you!" "Have you seen this?" "Do you remember that?" And so it went on. It became a lot of fun. When everybody had seen enough, all the sorted photos were again unsorted in one big messy pile, but I sorted them once more and put them in their envelopes to give to each child when they visited next. Some things are nice and important to save.

By making games and events with family and friends out of the difficult job of death cleaning photographs you have gathered over a long life, it can be less lonely, less overwhelming, and more fun. You also do not have to carry the weight of all those memories by yourself, and you are less likely to get stuck in the past.

STUFF YOU CAN'T GET RID OF

There are things that are difficult, almost impossible, to throw away, even when they seem useless and without value.

For example, when I was about to move to my two-room apartment, I discovered that I had forgotten a few family members, who sat there looking at me with sad glass eyes. They were our most beloved toy animals.

No one had thought of them for a long time, even though they had probably offered more joy and comfort than many human relatives. And I did not have small grandchildren to give them to anymore.

One grown-up grandchild took a few for their own children—among them Teddyfer (a very strange name, like a fluffy Lucifer), a big white polar bear that I got from my husband for Christmas when living in Singapore and that I used to dance with when he was not at home. And Ferdinam, a big blue hippo with a handle on his back, a tassel on his tail, and a striped beret on his head. I was glad that—like me—they were going to a new home, but I was sad to say good-bye.

Today, in my living room sits Dear Bumbal, a huge

koala bear that my husband brought from Australia. I believe he had a seat of his own on the flight. He sits there and looks very content. On a shelf in my bedroom sits The Old Bear. He looks just like Winnie-the-Pooh. He is a bit worn and wears a sweater and socks to keep the stuffing inside his body. But he is actually eighty years old. He has heard many little children's secrets and been a comfort and offered companionship for many years. Shall I throw him in the dump? No way. He will sit on his shelf with a few small friends for the time being.

THE "THROW AWAY" BOX

There are a few things that I would like to save for myself only. Things that make me remember events that I may forget otherwise. Old love letters, programs, memories from traveling. I have gathered all these personal things in a box that I have marked "Throw Away."

As you go through your papers, maybe you will find letters in which the writer calls you wonderful things such as "best and dearest friend," "delightful," or other nice things that you want to read again and would rather paper a wall with than throw away. When I find things like these, things that have absolutely no value to anyone else, but enormous value for me, I go and get my "Throw Away" box. Once I am gone, the box can be destroyed.

I know the first thing my children will do is check the contents of this box. But they can also choose not to. I have decided what others can throw away with a clean conscience. Although I imagine that some of the letters, pictures, and small things would amuse my dear ones if they do take a look before throwing the box away.

It is really very hard to do one's last cleaning. All the time I get stuck in different memories. At the same time, it is nice, in a way. I feel a certain relief when I decide to keep something small—a dried flower, a stone with a funny shape, or a little, beautiful shell—and put it in the "Throw Away" box. The box is for small things that are just valuable to me, as they remind me of special days and happenings.

It is very important that you do not choose a huge box—a shoe box should do.

CORRESPONDENCE AND COMMUNICATION

In our family, we have written lots and lots of letters. Mostly as a result of my husband's travels as a business-man for an international company. My mother-in-law used to complain, "My son is like a satellite—he is always moving and often so far away!"

As our family moved many times to places far away from Sweden, we kept in touch with our relatives and friends at home with letters. Telephone calls at that time were very expensive, and only used for very urgent messages. When the children grew older and visited friends, went on school trips, and later attended schools far away, they used to write cards or letters telling me and my husband what they were up to, or if they needed more money. I saved many of them.

Skype and FaceTime had not been invented yet so it took time and effort to keep in touch. Especially from countries far away in Africa or Asia with poorly developed communication systems. We had to be content that at least letters did not travel by boat or with couriers on horseback; at least they could travel by plane so as to arrive sooner.

I really do not know if my grandchildren can write at all. I mean with pen on paper. Nobody seems to do that anymore. I know that they are good at drawing, but considering the number of thank-you letters I have received during recent years, I am really not convinced that they even know how to write or if my presents to them ever arrived. As such, Facebook is a good thing: through it I can see that a present has arrived and maybe even that it was liked.

When our kids were young they had to sit down and write thank-you notes. Considering the effort someone had gone to in order to buy and send a present, and then the joy of receiving something, I think everybody felt it was worth the trouble.

When a child is too young to read and write in their own language, and then has to move to another country where they have to learn a new language, writing is a difficult task. Our youngest wanted to write to her friends at home just like her older sister and brothers did. She worked so hard and I heard how she sighed. Suddenly she said, "Mom, please write to them and say that I have died." She was only six years old at the time, but perhaps already knew that dying is a way of being let off the hook.

Much later I visited Malta where a grandchild talked with his Scandinavian friends through his computer. For hours! Free! And they played games together. And they laughed! Could he even imagine how his parents longed for that kind of contact forty years earlier?

For my mother-in-law, it was of course a terrible thing when her only child took his entire family to a country so far away that a weekend visit was out of the question.

So once a week I wrote a letter to her, telling her about our life and especially what her grandchildren were up to. She put all these letters in a blue plastic bag and gave them back to me when we returned home. A whole family diary! I am so happy for that bag today. And I am not going to throw it away. If I have time I will make five copies of each letter instead, and give them to each of my five children.

In case I do not have time to copy all the letters, I have marked every envelope with what it contains and who it is about. Like skating on the neighbor's pool, building a playhouse from a wooden container, or making a doll-house from a huge cardboard box, or parties, or making Christmas decorations.

WRITTEN THINGS

I have some very old cards, invitations, and letters. Some are more than two hundred years old. And they are really so well and carefully written, probably with that kind of pen that has to be dipped in ink all the time. Or maybe a goose feather, a "quill" I believe it is called. Written on very thin paper, now yellowed with age. They are really small pieces of art.

When I went to school, it was very important to write clearly and neatly. Today not many people write diaries or letters by hand. And if they do, the writing is sometimes hard to read—especially for those who have never felt how a pen moves in your hand when a letter is formed.

We had a class in my school called Writing. Most of us found it extremely boring. The teacher pestered us to write with ink pens that we had to dip in inkwells often. One time we got so fed up with him that we poured water in all the small ink bottles. That did not make our writing easier to read!

I have no major trouble reading other people's handwriting, but young people find it almost impossible to decipher other people's writing styles. I guess that maybe is why it is so hard for them to handwrite an answer in a letter. Of course it is much easier to sit down at the computer and click away something. It is fast and no envelope or postage is required. And you don't even have to visit a mailbox. But I still think that to receive a postcard in your mailbox is happiness!

A young team of filmmakers, including my daughter, is making a documentary on the great Swedish artist and film director Ingmar Bergman. They were having a hard time reading his handwritten diaries as they were written in a style from almost one hundred years ago, and

THE GENTLE ART OF SWEDISH DEATH CLEANING

called on me for assistance. It was not very easy for me to decipher, either, but it wasn't hell at least. Incidentally, I discovered that Ingmar Bergman thought about his death all the time, as is evident in some of his films, but didn't bother to do any death cleaning. In Stockholm we now have a huge Ingmar Bergman archive as a result. Perhaps sometimes it is not good to death clean—at least if you have made a great body of work.

I do not save the few and rare letters and cards I get anymore. As soon as I have answered and thanked the writers for them they disappear into my shredder. Only if a card is extremely funny or beautiful will I tape it on the door in my kitchen or I sometimes put it in my "Throw Away" box to revisit and enjoy again at a future moment.

MY LITTLE BLACK BOOK

Sometimes I wonder if the next generation will be able to read small notes or lovely and interesting messages that they have received and will receive from relatives and friends during the years.

I know that there are many ways to save everything you want to save in your computer. I have friends that do not have access to the Internet. They do not have a computer or an iPad or even a cell phone, and they have not bothered to do anything about it. Both men and women. This is very impractical. They say they can manage well without these modern inventions. Well, well, maybe so, but they are also deprived of a lot of important information that could make their days easier and more interesting. Sometimes I have the feeling that I live in a different world than some of my friends.

I do not understand how I would manage without the Internet. At least once a day I read and answer what has come into my mailbox. It may be a simple question, an invitation, or a regular letter, and of course some advertising that I would like to erase. I might look for an address or a telephone number, pay my bills, buy tickets to a movie or a train or a plane ticket when I want to go somewhere.

And if there are TV programs that I did not have the opportunity to watch, I can look at them on my computer at a time that is more convenient for me. You can buy almost anything. You can use it as a dictionary, as a cookbook, and much more.

Technology advances so fast that it is sometimes hard to keep pace, especially for us elderly. Not only because we are slower than we used to be, but also because we forget things quickly and have to listen and learn all over again. This is of course very annoying and tiring. You have to write down many things. That is so very important when you use your computer. To enter certain websites you sometimes have to use a password. Over time the number of passwords you have swells and swells. They are too many to remember, even for young people.

I have a small black book with a red back. In this little book I keep all my passwords so that I can get access to everything I want in my computer. And when the day comes, when I am somewhere else, my family can easily find what they need.

It is nice that the Internet has made it easy to communicate, but in a way I think it is sad that so many written words and thoughts just disappear into the air. Who saves text messages in an old cell phone? How many old cell phones would you have to keep in order to preserve some of your most precious texts? And all the chargers to all these cell phones if you want to read a message. Impossible. This is another problem with the advancement of technology. All the gadgets that at one moment are a must, and the next moment completely useless.

I have tried to keep up with the times, and also do away with the old. When our eight-track cassettes from the seventies became outdated, I threw them away. The same goes for my videotapes—I had them digitized, then threw them away. With my LPs it was different. A son-in-law collects vinyl and picked out a few that he wanted. The rest I threw away.

It goes without saying that I have also gotten rid of the outdated tape recorders and turntables we played our music on.

While a beautiful art deco toaster from the 1920s can be pleasant to look at today, I think very few of our gadgets, chargers, routers, etc., will be admired in the future.

DEATH CLEANING IS AS MUCH (OR MORE!) FOR YOU AS FOR THE PEOPLE WHO COME AFTER

I have already made the point that death cleaning is something you should do so that your children and other loved ones will not have to deal with all your stuff.

While I think this motivation is a very important one, it is not the full story.

Death cleaning is also something you can do for yourself, for your own pleasure. And if you start early, at say sixty-five, it won't seem like such a huge task when you, like me, are between eighty and one hundred.

One's own pleasure, and the chance to find meaning and memory, is the most important thing. It is a delight to go through things and remember their worth. And if you don't remember why a thing has meaning or why you kept it, it has no worth, and it will be easier for you to part with.

Today, I meet many relatively young people who do not have children of their own.

One might think, Well, I have no children, therefore I need not death clean. Wrong.

Someone will have to clean up after you. Whoever it may be will find it a burden.

Our planet is very small; it floats in a never-ending universe. It may perish under the weight of our consumerism— and eventually I fear that it will. If you have no children of your own, you should still be sure to death clean both for the pleasure it can bring you, but also for all the other children out there who you don't know. Recycling and donating can both help the planet and also bring things to people who may need them.

One of my children who has no children of her own has a huge collection of books. This child (fifty by now) is desperately trying to find a young person who likes to read, in order to give away some of the books. Her collection is wonderful. She has always been a reader, and many of the books from me and from my husband's parents have ended up in her library.

Most people will, if they look hard enough, find someone to give their things to. If you don't have children, you might have siblings, and nieces or nephews. Or you have friends, coworkers, neighbors who may be happy to receive your possessions.

If you cannot find anyone to give your possessions to, sell them and make a donation to charity. If you don't death clean and show people what is valuable, once you die there will be a big truck that takes all the wonderful things you have to an auction (at best) or a dump. No one will be happy about that. Well, the auction house might be.

So if you do not have children of your own, you still have a duty to sort out your life. Go through your items, remember them, give them away. There is always a young person starting a new life, starting a new home, wanting to read everything written by Somerset Maugham (I admit this one is rare). You don't have to be a blood relative to give them pots and pans, chairs from your attic, an old rug. When these young people can afford to purchase exactly what they want, they will pass your old furniture on to their friends, and then to their friends, and so on. You cannot know the places your objects may go after you are gone and that could be wonderful to contemplate.

If you give an old desk to a young person, make a story

about it, not a lie of course, but tell them what kind of letters were written on it, what documents were signed, what types of thoughts were entertained around this desk—and the story will grow as it is passed on from young person to younger person to younger person. An ordinary desk becomes extraordinary through time.

One of my friends was given a desk by a friend who was leaving Stockholm. It was from the 1700s. We admire this desk now. We sit and write at it, and always wonder what has been written on it. Who wrote sitting there hundreds of years ago? What were they writing? Why were they writing it? And to whom? A love letter? A business deal? A confession?

It is a beautiful desk; we all appreciate this. But more than its beauty, it has been in use for three hundred years. I wish everyone who wrote on it had left a record. My friend has written a small note and tucked it inside. She will sell it soon. I hope the tradition carries on.

THE STORY OF ONE'S LIFE

Death cleaning is certainly not just about things. If it were, it would not be so difficult.

Although our belongings can bring many memories to

life, it becomes more difficult with photographs and written words.

They are all about feelings! Going through letters is very time-consuming—you will get stuck in old memories and perhaps dream yourself back to old times. That may be nice and bring you happy memories, but it may also move you in other ways, bringing up sad and even depressing feelings.

I have both laughed and cried reading through my old letters. Occasionally I regretted saving some of them. There were things I had forgotten and then suddenly it all came back. Again! But if you want to see the whole picture of your story and your life, even less funny things have to show up.

The more I have focused on my cleaning, the braver I have become. I often ask myself, Will anyone I know be happier if I save this? If after a moment of reflection I can honestly answer no, then it goes into the hungry shredder, always waiting for paper to chew. But before it goes into the shredder, I have had a moment to reflect on the event or feeling, good or bad, and to know that it has been a part of my story and of my life.

AFTER LIFE

It is hard for me to understand why most people find death so difficult to talk about. It is the only absolutely inevitable happening that we all have in our future.

How we would prefer to arrange things if we fall ill and how we want to be treated when we are dead are decisions that are within our power, if we face and take control of these inevitabilities. I know very well that we sometimes need professional help to go forward. Perhaps from a lawyer to draw up a will. But I am not qualified to give legal advice—I am just a death cleaner.

There are so many options about how we can think about and prepare for our own departure from life. No choice is wrong. Some wish to be cremated and have their ashes spread at sea; some want to be buried in a coffin. And of course there are many other things about one's death and funeral to think about. To spare your relatives and others from all these difficult decisions, you can actually decide it all by yourself while you are still able to do so. Talk to someone close about your wishes or write them down. Just try to be practical!

In this book I wanted to get you started with your cleaning and make you feel good when you think of all the hours you will have saved your loved ones, because they will not have to use their precious time to take care of stuff you do not want yourself anymore.

I will feel so content and happy when I have done most of this work. Maybe I can still manage to travel somewhere, or buy myself flowers and invite some friends to a nice dinner to celebrate all the work done. And if I don't die, I will probably go shopping. Again!

APPENDIX:
THREE RECIPES FROM
ANDRÉA IN BOHUSLÄN

PICKLED ROSEHIP MARMALADE

2¼ pounds (1 kg) rosehip berries
2½ cups (6 ml) water
½ cup plus 2 tablespoons (1½ dl) white vinegar
2½ cups (500 g) sugar
5 to 10 whole cloves
1 cinnamon stick, crushed

Cut the berries in half and scoop out the insides with a small spoon.

Heat the water, vinegar, sugar, and spices in a saucepan and bring to a boil. Add the well-cleaned berries and continue to boil until the berries are soft. Strain out the cloves and crushed cinnamon stick. Pour into jars and close the lids.

MARGARETA MAGNUSSON

RED BEET SHERRY

2¼ pounds (1 kg) beetroots
1 gallon (4 l) water
10 cups (2 kg) sugar
1 package (250 g) raisins
3½ ounces (100 g) yeast
2 slices rye or other bread (do not use white bread)

Boil the beets in the water until soft. Retain the water and pour it into a bowl. Add the sugar and raisins. Spread the yeast on the bread slices as you might butter a sandwich. Place the bread slices on top of the beet liquid. Cover and let stand for 1 month. Stir now and then (about once a week). Strain and pour into a bottle. Enjoy!

BOHUSLÄN CHEESECAKE

1 gallon (4 l) milk
2½ cups (6 dl) heavy cream
1½ cups plus 3 tablespoons (400 ml) buttermilk
8 to 10 eggs
3½ tablespoons (45 g) sugar (optional—should only be used if making as a dessert)

Mix all the ingredients except the sugar in a big saucepan. Heat it very slowly and stir constantly from the bottom with a wooden spatula. Do not let it boil. You have to watch the mixture carefully. When it becomes grainy, put the saucepan aside and let it rest for 5 to 10 minutes. Heat it up one more time but do not boil!

Spoon the mixture into a cheesecake mold or cake pan that has little holes in it so that the excess liquid can drain off. If you are making a dessert, sprinkle some sugar between the layers of the mixture as you spoon it in. Or you can layer it in without adding sugar. Let it rest for about 4 hours.

Without sugar it is eaten together with pickled herring or smoked salmon. As a dessert, the cheesecake with the sugar is very good with blackberry jam.

ACKNOWLEDGMENTS

I want to thank Stephen Morrison for inspiring me to write this book and giving me so much friendly advice along the way.

Also, I would like to thank my publishers, Nan Graham and Kara Watson at Scribner, and Jamie Byng, Jenny Todd, and Hannah Knowles at Canongate and Henry Rosenbloom at Scribe for their thoughtful input, which made my book so much better. I also want to thank Susanna Lea for her hard work and for a wonderful lunch in Stockholm, and to her incredible team: Laura, Mark, Cece, Kerry, and Lauren, who have made this ride so pleasantly smooth.

And lastly I would like to thank my daughter Jane and her husband, Lars. Without them, this book would never have come about.

ABOUT THE AUTHOR

I have been asked for my biography! Do I have one?

I know I was born in Gothenburg, Sweden, on New Year's Eve. That was good timing! As a child I thought that it was because of me and my day of birth that all the church bells rang, all the boats in the harbor blew their horns, and the fireworks crackled and sparkled in the sky.

My parents loved me, even when I screamed. My father was a doctor; my mother stayed home and organized the life they led. At that time it was very common for women to stay home full-time, even though she had been educated as a nurse.

I went to a nonreligious, coed school starting at age

seven. After I graduated from high school, I was admitted to Beckman's College of Design in Stockholm. When I'd finished my program there, it was easy for me to get a job because the school was well regarded, but it was hard for me to choose what I wanted to do. I found work as a fashion and advertisement designer at a large department store that sold everything except food and stationery.

When the children started to arrive, I began working from home, delivering drawings while carrying a baby in a basket. I also painted a lot with oil and watercolors and ink. My first solo exhibition was in Gothenburg in 1979. Later I had more shows in Stockholm, Singapore, and Hong Kong and many other places in Sweden, too. When a painting in a gallery has been sold, it is the custom to put a round red sticker on the wall next it. At a number of these gallery shows, I sold so many paintings that we joked that the gallery had caught the measles. I enjoyed my career as an artist and still enjoy painting and drawing. I think I will keep my brushes, drawing papers, and paints till the end.

I have had such fun, but now that I am aged somewhere between eighty and one hundred, I am getting a little tired and want to slow down.

I have collected many things over the years, and it gives me such joy to go through them all. Sorting through everything is sad sometimes, too, but I really do not want to give my beloved children and their families too much trouble with my stuff after I am gone. That is why I want to tell others about death cleaning, and how wonderful and challenging it can be!